Two Blue Cockatoos

a book about rhyme

Ruth Thomson

Belitha Press

First published in the UK in 2000 by
Belitha Press Ltd
A member of Chrysalis Books Plc.
64 Brewery Road, London N7 9NT

Copyright © Belitha Press Ltd 2000
Text copyright © Ruth Thomson 2000
Illustrations © Belitha Press 2000

All rights reserved. No part of this book may be reproduced or utilized in
any form or by any means, electronic or mechanical, including photocopying,
recording or by any information storage and retrieval system, except by
a reviewer, who may quote brief passages in a review.

ISBN 1 84138 203 5 (hardback)
ISBN 1 84138 211 6 (paperback)
ISBN 1 84138 232 9 (big book)

British Library in Publication Data for this book is available
from the British Library.

Series editors: Mary-Jane Wilkins, Stephanie Turnbull
Designers: Rachel Hamdi, Holly Mann, Angie Allison
Illustrators: Patrice Aggs, Louise Comfort, Brenda Haw, Holly Mann
Educational consultants: Pie Corbett, Poet and Consultant
   to the National Literacy Strategy; Sarah Mullen, Literacy Consultant

Printed in Hong Kong
hb:10 9 8 7 6 5 4 3 2 1   pb:10 9 8 7 6 5 4 3 2

Two Blue Cockatoos

a book about rhyme

This beautiful book will help to lay the early foundations for reading and writing. Young children love words and often invent their own, savouring the sounds. They will enjoy the rhyming games in the book.

Some are games that help children listen carefully and identify rhymes. This is essential to early reading and spelling. Other pages focus upon hearing the sounds at the beginning, at the end or in the middle of words. This is vital for early spelling.

Early play with sounds, rhymes and letters should be fun – and is fundamental to becoming a reader. Children are never too young to enjoy words, to begin listening carefully to sounds or to notice letters. These games will make the pathway to reading and writing both simple and joyful.

Pie Corbett

Pie Corbett

Poet and Consultant to the National Literacy Strategy

There are extra activities to reinforce children's learning on page 31. On page 32 you will find a list of the rhyming words pictured on pages 4-5 and 18-30.

Turn the key. Undo the locks.
Find some words that rhyme with box.

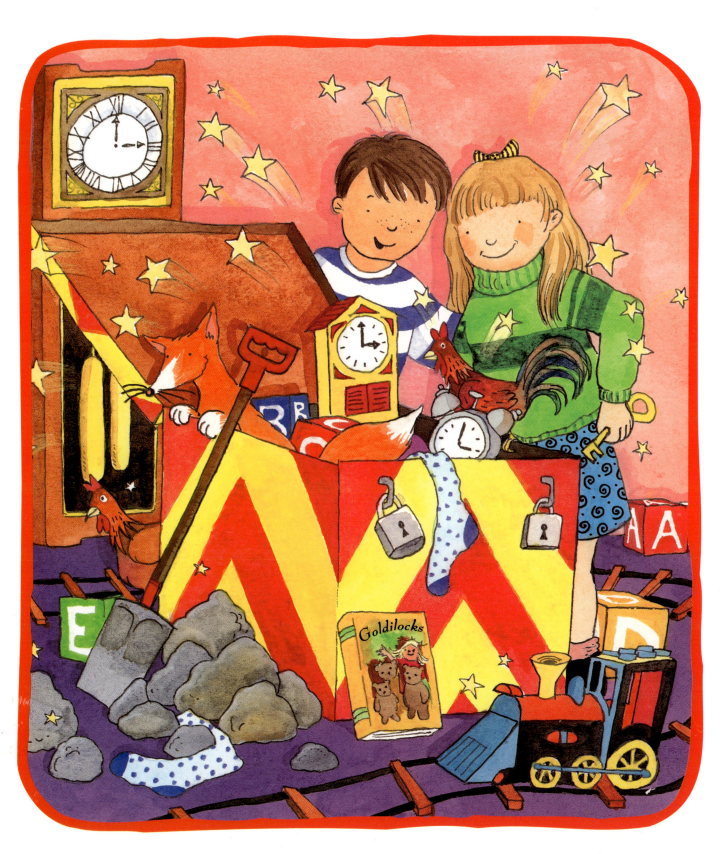

I spy with my little eye
Someone here who waves goodbye.

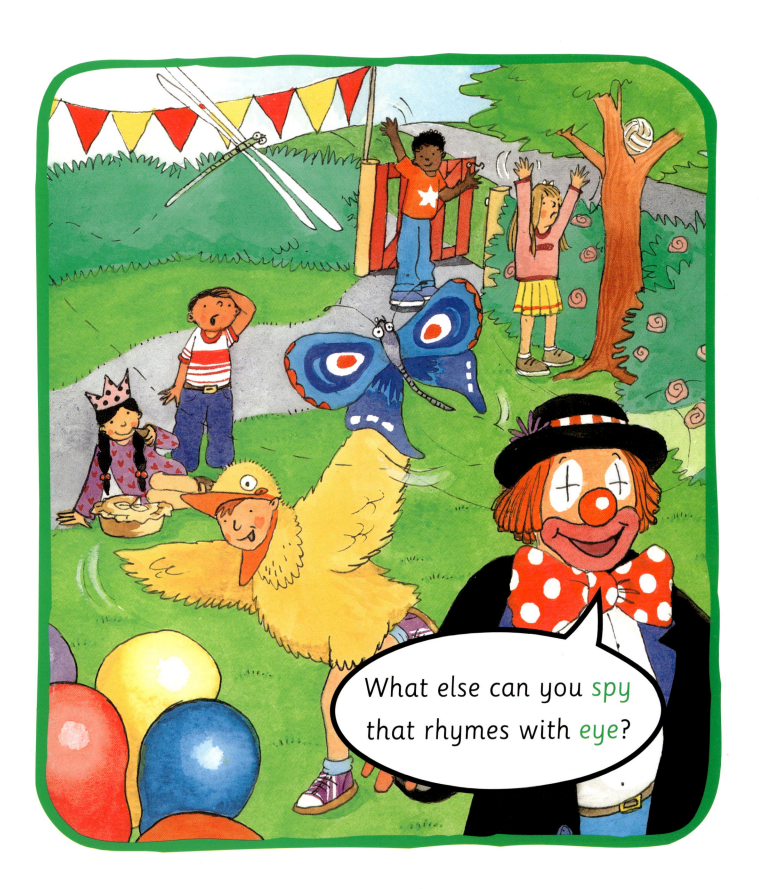

Ready, steady, go.
Tell me what you know.

Find the rhyming words to finish these couplets.

Ready, steady, go.

I can point my...

finger

wand

toe

Ready, steady, go.

The boys have gone to...

swim   row

climb

Ready, steady, go.

I can tie...

a bow

a knot

my laces

Ready, steady, go.

It's time for you to…

clap

blow

wave

Ready, steady, go.

The gardener has to…

rake

weed

mow

Ready, steady, go.

The cock begins to…

crow

eat

sleep

Ready, steady, go.

The mirror is too…

high

low

crooked

One, two, buckle my shoe.
Three, four, knock on the door.
Five, six, pick up sticks.
Seven, eight, open the gate.
Nine, ten, start over again.

Choose some rhyming words to make your own rhymes.

One, two...

wait in a queue

paint the door green

eat a banana

blue cockatoo

catch a big fish

wash my dog with shampoo

Three, four...

jump in the air

lie on the floor

shells on the shore

hear the lion roar

blow up a balloon

hear grandpa snore

Five, six...

small fluffy chicks

fly a bright kite

do magic tricks

practise some kicks

build with toy bricks

ride my new bike

Seven, eight...

cake on a plate

bounce a big ball

brush my long hair

lift up a weight

put on my skate

carry a crate

Nine, ten...

write with a pen

keep out of my den

ring a big bell

two silly men

sit on a chair

a little black hen

Roses are red.
Violets are blue.
Sugar is sweet.
And so are you.

Think of a word to finish these rhymes.
Use the pictures to help you.

Tomatoes are red.
Spiders are black.
Don't look behind you.
There's one on your...

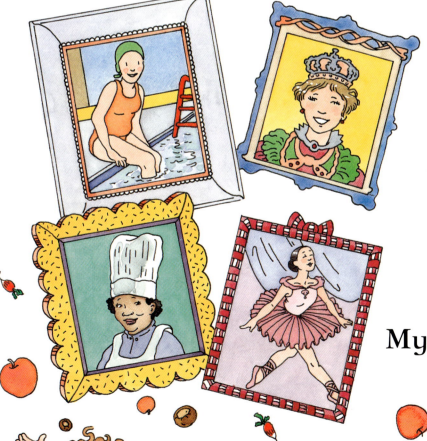

Apples are red.
A cabbage is green.
My dad is a drummer.
My mum is a...

A radish is red.
A conker is brown.
My dad wears white trainers.
My mum wears a...

Monday's child...

Choose the rhyming food words to finish this poem.

Monday's child adores fresh peas.

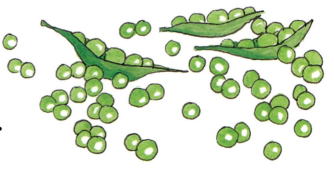

Tuesday's child prefers sliced...

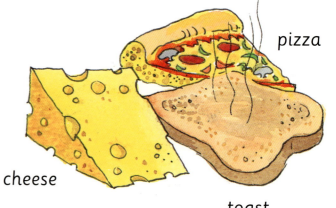

pizza

cheese

toast

 Wednesday's child eats all her greens.

 Thursday's child likes hot…

hamburger
fried egg
baked beans

 Friday's child enjoys French fries.

Saturday's child loves…

apple pies   ice cream   chocolate cake

And the child that is born on the seventh day scoffs the lot.
Hip hip hooray!

Teddy bear, teddy bear

Find the rhyming words to finish these couplets.

Teddy bear, teddy bear,
turn around.
Teddy bear, teddy bear,

Teddy bear, teddy bear,
touch your toes.
Teddy bear, teddy bear,

lie on the bed

make a sound

dig the ground

what have you found?

pat your nose

hold the hose

smell a rose

sail your boat

Teddy bear, teddy bear,
nod your head.
Teddy bear, teddy bear,

eat your bread

go to bed

brush your teeth

lock your shed

Teddy bear, teddy bear,
fly your kite.
Teddy bear, teddy bear,

put out the light

wash your face

wave good night

take a bite

Ten little monkeys

Choose the right words to finish these rhymes.

One little monkey hiding in a tree.
Two little monkeys splashing in the...

puddle

bath

sea

Three little monkeys hiding in the dark.
Four little monkeys playing in the...

sandpit

park

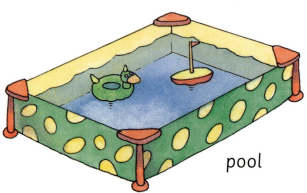
pool

16

Five little monkeys drinking lemonade.
Six little monkeys digging with a…

spoon

spade

fork

Seven little monkeys chasing pussy cats.
Eight little monkeys wearing stripy…

caps

hats

gloves

Nine little monkeys nodding little heads.
Ten little monkeys sleeping in their…

chairs

cots

beds

B Betty Botter bought a bit of butter.

Choose other things for Betty to buy that start with the same sound.

P p

Peter Piper paints pictures of peacocks in the park.

Find more things starting with the same sound that Peter Piper could paint.

R r

Around the rugged rock the ragged rascal ran.

What else can you see that starts with the same sound?

S s

Simon saw seven snakes slither under the sofa.

Find some other things in the picture that start with the same sound.

n # The tin man can spin
a pan on his chin. n

What else can you see
that ends in n?

t One starry, moonlit night, I saw a funny sight. t

I am a rat in a hat.

What else can you see that ends in t?

d　Guess what dad said when we hid in his shed?　d

What else is in the shed that ends with d?

ee   ee

Fi-fo-fiddle-dee-dee
I see an elephant stuck up a tree.

What else can you see that rhymes
with fi-fo-fiddle-dee-dee?

a Rat-a-tat-tat! Whoever is that?
The man, the rat or the cat? a

What else can you see that
has an a sound in the middle?

e 'H**e**lp! H**e**lp!' w**e**pt poor M**e**g. e
'No h**e**ns in the sh**e**d!'

What else can you see that
has an e sound in the middle?

i Ding-a-ling! Bill rings his bell as he whizzes down the hill. i

What else can you see that has an i sound in the middle?

H**o**ppity-fl**o**p. The fr**o**g h**o**ps fr**o**m m**o**ssy r**o**ck to r**o**tten l**o**g.

What else can you see that has an o sound in the middle?

u The dump truck is stuck in the sludgy mud. u

What else can you see that has an u sound in the middle?

Notes for parents and teachers

These games will help children to identify sounds at the beginning, middle and end of words, which leads on to recognition of rhyme.

Odd one out

Choose a group of words with the same initial sound and include one with a different sound, eg star, sock, soap, coat. Ask children to identify the odd word out. Help them by exaggerating the initial sound. Repeat the game with end sounds then middle sounds. Once children can identify initial sounds they will quickly move on to recognizing end sounds, but it may be several weeks before they can recognize middle sounds.

Pass the sound

The children sit in a circle. Say a word which begins with an easily identifiable initial sound, eg m – mouse. The child next to you then thinks of a word beginning with the same sound, and so on around the circle. Once they have mastered this, move on to end, middle and rhyming sounds.

Pairs

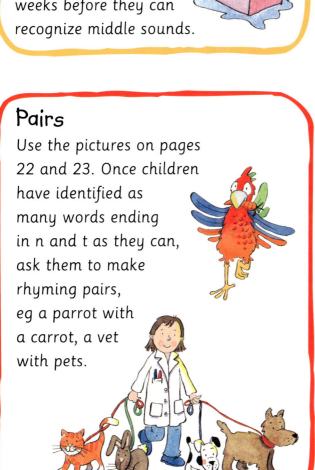

Use the pictures on pages 22 and 23. Once children have identified as many words ending in n and t as they can, ask them to make rhyming pairs, eg a parrot with a carrot, a vet with pets.

Silly puppet

This game encourages children to hear and identify sounds at the ends of words. You need a glove puppet, small toys or everyday objects and a bag to put them in. The glove puppet takes one item at a time out of the bag and says its name with the wrong end sound. For example, if the object is a dog, the puppet says, 'This is my doll, dot, dock, dosh,' (the sillier the name the better) and the children finish the word correctly for the puppet.

31

Word list

Here are the words to find in this book.

page 4
building blocks
clocks
cocks
fox
Goldilocks
locks
rocks
socks

page 5
bow tie
butterfly
dragonfly
(trying to) fly
(reaching) high
pie
sky

page 18
babies' bibs
bags
balls
bananas
 (in a bunch)
baskets
beads
beakers
beans
bees
bells
belts
blue (jumper)
boots
bottles
bowls
bows
boxes
bracelets
brown (ball)
buckets
buckles
building bricks
bulbs

butterflies
buttons

page 19
paddling pool
paintbrush
palace (pink)
palette
paper
 (a piece of)
parrots
 (purple)
path
peaches
pears
pencil
people
picnic
pie (in pieces)
pigeons
pillow
pineapple
plants
plates
 (in a pile)
plums (purple)
pond
ponytail
pram (being
 pushed)
puppy (pulling
 on a lead)

page 20
rabbits
raccoon
racing car
rat
rattlesnake
referee
robot (rusty)
roller skates
rooster (red)
rucksack

page 21
sail
sailing boat
sandwiches
saxophone
scarf (striped)
sea
seaside
seat
sitting room
skier
skis
slippers
snail
snakes (silver,
 spotted,
 striped and
 speckled)
snow
snowman
socks
soup
spaghetti
spider
spoon
spots
squash
squirrel
stairs
starfish
stool
straw
strawberries
stripes
sun
surfboard
surfer
swan

page 22
bin
crown
fan
green (dress)

hen
iron
man
pen
queen
twin
van

page 23
boat
boot
carrot
ghost
goat
knight
light
newt
parrot
pet
toast
vet
white (armour)

page 24
bed
bedstead
bird
bread
cupboard
pea pod
rod
surfboard
thread
wood

page 25
bee
key
knee
monkey
sea
tea
three

page 26
back
bat
black
cap
Dan
fan
hand
hat
lad
latch
mat
pan
patch
sack
sand

page 27
bed
belt
bench
check
dress
fence
hedge
leg
men
net
peck
red
shed (red
 and yellow)
shelf
step
ten
tent

page 28
bricks
bridge
builders
chicks
dig
grin

grip
pig
pink
stick
swing
twigs
windmill
zip

page 29
blonde
blossom
box
clogs
dog
doll
donkey
fox
padlock
pond
pot
rod
spot

page 30
brush
chubby
drum
duck
grubby
gull
hung
hut
jumper
mug
plump
rug
scrub
stump
sun